Content Marketing Strategies

How Delivering Sensational Value
Can Help You Build A Digital Media
Empire

COPYRIGHT

Disclaimer

FREE GIFT
Kindle 5 Star Books

Free Kindle 5 Star Book Club Membership

Join Other Kindle 5 Star Members Who Are Getting Private Access To Weekly
Free Kindle Book Promotions

Get free Kindle books

Stay connected:
Join our Facebook group
Follow Kindle 5 Star on Twitter

Also, if you want to receive updates on Entrepreneur Publishing's new books, free
promotions and Kindle countdown deals sign up to their New Release Mailing
List.

For entrepreneurs: http://www.entrepreneurfinesse.com

Table of Contents

Introduction

If you are a website owner, a business person or an online marketer, this book was written especially for you. This book was written for you in mind if you are looking to improve the overall content quality of your website and to improve not only your visitor engagement on your site, but also to improve your overall website traffic.

In this book you will find a variety of chapters that will give you the ultimate secrets that you need to generate the content that you need to benefit your website. You will also find a variety of techniques and methods that you can use to reach your target audience and engage them in ways that you have never thought of before.

When you equip yourself with all of the tools you need to write engaging and high quality content to have success in the online and marketing world. Hopefully by the books end you will gain a much better understand and knowledge you need to achieve the best content marketing success.

So, without further ado, let's get started!

Chapter One: What Is The Value of Successful Content On Your Website?

Basically, the internet was created as a source of information. Thus, if you own a website, it must provide relevant and important contents for your audience. If the content on your website doesn't provide the information that your users want, then it will be of little value to your site visitors who surf the internet.

Are you someone who always post a new blog or article on your website just to add something new and fresh, and then wonder why you miss out new readers and web traffic?

Well you have to keep in mind that people are visiting blogs and websites because they're looking for information. They often require solutions or answers to their problems, wants, needs and desires. If you want to gain new readers and have your existing ones return again and again, then provide them something relevant and valuable.

Why Is Content The Most Important Aspect of Your Website?

Websites are valuable platforms to communicate effectively whatever message you want to get across your audience. If you want to achieve success in any of your online endeavor, you have to answer the questions of your visitors or satisfy their need for information and knowledge.

In order to achieve this, you will need a website that is rich with useful content. The content of your website must be up to date, well organized, relevant and written uniquely on every page of the website. Your web content must also be written as if you're talking to your audience.

How To Make Your Content Useful and Informative

In order to write informative and valuable posts, you need first to know the issues your audience are dealing with, the problems they are facing, the questions they are asking, their needs, wants and desires. After identifying these things, it is the time for you to research and determine your niche.

To do this, you can find some of the most popular websites within your niche. Such sites can provide you with some valuable insight about your potential customers. This will also help you determine their age group, location, income level and even their gender.

You can now write based on the data gathered. Of course, you're not going to write in similar manner for a group of young adult males as you would for senior males. Your choice of language, general advice and tone must be according to the information obtained.

If you want to know the problems your readers face, visit some forums. Note their questions, and write a post or an article to answer them.

Some of the things you need to do to are:

1. Write tutorials, tips and unique articles that will draw the attention and get the interest of your visitors and get them to return to your website.

2. Always update your content to keep the website interesting and fresh. If you want to have good traffic, keep in mind that major Search Engines always look for websites that offer useful information.

3. Avoid the use of jargon when writing web content. Use only familiar words.

4. Make your content Search Engine friendly by making a content rich site that contains texts instead of images.

5. Consider your website design. It must attract both the Search Engines and visitors.

Indeed, content marketing is one of the best marketing approaches you should use to obtain your online endeavors and reach an increased number of clients. Whether you have an online business or a personal blog, having a content-rich website is important to achieve online success.

Chapter Two: The Best Places To Use Your Content And Find Readers

So, where can you actually use content?

When you hear the term "content", what comes into your mind? Some people would often associate content with putting posts and articles on their blogs and websites. Well, this is absolutely right, but there are some other places where you will need relevant contents too.

Is your website linked to common social media websites like Google Plus, Twitter, LinkedIn, Facebook or Instagram? Do you have an account to any of these popular Social Media Sites?

If you don't, then you actually should. The best way to increase traffic to your site and find new online readers is by sharing your posts to different social pages.

How To Take Advantage of The Power of Social Media

There are millions of Facebook users today throughout the world, and most of them spend long hours browsing through their social medial accounts. There are also millions of Tweets being done every day. If you want to increase the number of your audience, maximize the power of different social media sites.

If you still do not have an account to any of these social media sites, it is the right time to make one. A lot of businesses have obtained success through these sites, and if you want to have introduce your business to more people, you have to take advantage of these sites.

Obviously, you need useful content for these websites. This is often something that holds people back from linking their social media websites into their marketing plans.

How Do You Get Ideas For Your Content?

This might be something that hinders you from connecting your business site to your social media site. The process seems to be daunting, causing you too much stress and anxiety. In order to relieve stress, you have to understand that it is actually not as difficult as you might think.

This can actually be as simple as saying. "I just recently wrote an article, check it out and feel free to share it with others."

If you are not good at writing or you really hate writing, you can always install a social sharing plugin on your website. When you blog post is already published, you can now share across your different social media accounts. In doing so, there is no need for you to write new contents at all.

But, if you want to make fresh and new contents for your social media sites, you could write a summary or a brief description/ discussion of your first article. Or maybe, you may just post its quick snippet.

For some social websites like Twitter, you have to condense every paragraph into a sentence, since the character length is very limited. You may also need new content to make slides or make videos. You can post this content to places, including YouTube and many different slide sharing websites.

You do not need entirely new content in doing this. You can just use the first article you have written and then make slides out of it.

As you can see, there are many different places where you can use your content. Just make sure that you are able to achieve your marketing purpose in all of these sites.

Chapter Three: How To Find Your Voice and Find Your Target Customer

One of the first things you need to do before writing any content is identify the audience for whom you're creating it. This will help you to not only figure out what topics to cover but also what form of content will best reach this audience (video, pictures, etc.). To uncover this information, you need to create a user profile and persona. A profile describes the overall characteristics of the target audience while personas are more like illustrations of virtual users; they are created based on data collected from user research on real users. More importantly, however, personas represent behavior patterns and motivations.

1. User Profile

User profiles are based on a list of characterizations about your users, and each business might have a different list that is important to them. You can get lots of this data from a variety of sources such as: your customer list, website analytics, Facebook insights page, etc. The following is a short list of some broad characteristics you can use to identify your customers, but each business is different and other characteristics might be important such as:

-Age
-Location
-Income
-Gender
-Computer Skill
-Culture
-Language
-Disabilities

2. User Persona

A persona is a fictional character created to represent the different types that typically use your product or service. Creating personas is useful in helping you consider the goals, behaviors and desires of your customers and they help guide you in the creation of your content. Personas are typically created from data gathered during interviews with your existing customer base.

You can create a simple, one -page description that includes their goals, attitudes, skills, and behavioral patterns with a few fictional personal details to make the character come alive. Companies will usually make a few different personas for each product within their product line. One persona is usually considered the primary persona for each given product. Adding a human face to your customers usually makes it easier to write and produce content for them and gives everyone in your organization a better understanding of your target customer.

Chapter Four: Types of Content That You Can Write

Teaching Others About Your Particular Product or Service

One of the basic pillars of effective content marketing is teaching about your product or service. Your product can range from the simple to the complex to understand. Regardless of where your product falls on the scale, producing content that teaches consumers about your product is an amazing way to get people to understand and buy your product or service.

If you are selling a complex product or service to other businesses, try and take into account all the people from different departments that will be involved in the decision process . As an example, imagine you're selling online recruiting software. It's obvious that the human resources department will be using this software, but take into account that every department in the company might also be using this software in a more limited capacity. Think about how you might explain this software to all the different departments that might use this software.

Regardless of where you fall on the scale of complexity, try and figure out how you can educate the consumer about your product.

Entertainment Content

Making your customers laugh, sing along with joy, and touching their hearts is an amazing way to connect your brand with your customers. Nothing tears down our guard faster than experiencing an emotion through some form of content. People don't remember facts and figures, but they do remember a great story and they love to share those stories with friends.

There are many ways to entertain while selling at the same time. The use of videos, pictures, and sounds allow you to connect with your customers in a very different and emotional way from many other types of content. Remember to think about your audience and try and figure out what's most important in their lives. Use social media to discover their likes and preferences and try to match them.

Utilities and Applications Content

When people first think of content marketing, they often think about blog posts, videos and funny pictures. Another great approach is providing tools and utilities to your clients; it's an easy way to get them to visit your site when they need your product the most.

A class example is a bank offering a mortgage calculator on its site. This allows consumers to figure out what their mortgage payment would be on a house but it also allows banks to brand themselves when someone is early in the mortgage process. These days' people aren't always on their computers, so offering a free mobile application of the same tool is a great way to reach out to consumers. This Zillow mortgage calculator is the first one that comes up in the Apple App store. It's well done and has great reviews from almost 350 people.

Every industry is different but try and think about the tools that your clients use to make their decisions. Try to provide these tools and get involved in their decision-making process early.

How To Curate Your Content Appropriately

Nearly 95 percent of marketers doing content marketing now use some form of content aggregation according to the Content Curation Adoption Survey 2012. This involves the process of constantly finding, organizing, and sharing highly relevant content that caters to your audience. Of those surveyed, 85 percent believe this helps establish them as thought leaders within their industry.

Most content aggregators blend company-generated materials with third-party content. Social media channels are important for all content aggregators as 79 percent use social media to find new sources of content and about the same number of people use it to distribute that content.

You can start off by using a few simple tools that make finding content easier.

1. Using Newsfeeds

RSS feeds are one of the easiest ways to receive targeted content from a specific website. Some very large sites also have individual RSS feeds for categories within their site.

2. Google Alerts

Google Alerts allows you to set up search terms that will automatically run at selected intervals that search news sources throughout the web.

3. Google Blog Search

Google Blog Search allows you to search for a large number of blogs and maybe find a few new ones. You can have Google Alerts search blogs as well, but you can use this at times when you are looking for new blogs you might want to add it to an RSS feed.

4. All Top

All Top imports the stories from the tops news websites and blogs for any given topic and displays the headlines of the five most recent stories. It's a good place to see what's going on at a glance on a certain topic.

5. Social Media

There are a ton of people and companies in your industry that is currently on Facebook, Twitter, LinkedIn and other social media website that share great stories about a variety of topics. These people are also a good source for news.

Chapter Five: Types of Content Portals You Can Have

1. A Corporate Website

Your corporate website should be the backbone of your content marketing strategy. When possible, you should always strive to drive traffic to your own personal website. To do this, you should always keep it alive with fresh content. These days, updating a website isn't as difficult as it was even five years ago. With the advent of content management systems (CMS) like WordPress, it's very easy to update a website on a daily basis.

Having A Company Blog

A blog is a type of website or part of a website that is usually arranged in chronological order from the most recent "post" (or story) at the top of the main page to the older entries toward the bottom. A blog can be written by a single person (sometimes called a blogger) or a team of people and should be updated frequently. Blogs generally cover a single topic and, in the case of a corporate blog, a company or industry. The obscure topics of some blogs would amaze you.

Typically, when you visit a blog, you are shown only the latest stories and you might not realize the huge archive of past articles that it contains. Over time these archives can be quite large if you've been a busy blogger. They can also be a great source to continue generating traffic from search engines.

One of the things you need to decide when creating a blog is if you're going to allow comments on your posts. There can be both pros and cons to allowing comments. By allowing them, you can help to generate a sense of community on your website. The con is that they need to be monitored on a continual basis to make sure that the comments align with your corporate goals. Usually, this is something that needs to be discussed internally and may depend on your industry. Blog posts can be anything from a long article about the state of your industry to photos from the company Christmas party. The one thing I would say about blogs though is if you're going to set up a blog, make sure you're going to commit to writing on a schedule. There is nothing worse than going to a corporate blog whose last entry was in 1999.

2. eBooks or White Papers

A white paper is a report or guide that helps readers understand a particulate topic. Typically, B2B marketers use them as a sales tool. They can contain research findings , survey results, or tips about an issue, and they can feature particular products or services from a vendor. Most of the time, users are required to register their e-mail to receive a particular white paper, and the user can be sent additional marketing materials.

The three most popular types of white papers are:

Backgrounder

These typically describe the technical and/or business benefits for your product or service. They are good tools to use to explain an unfamiliar or misunderstood product to your audience.

Numbered List

These are the fastest and easiest type of white paper to create. They are easy reads that provide a simple overview of a topic. You also use them to introduce fear, uncertainty and doubt into an industry marketplace.

Solution/Problem

These are often the ones that generate the most leads at the top of a sales funnel. They describe a problem within your industry that went unsolved until your product or service was released. They use facts, figures and logic to promote your new solution.

eBooks are book-length publications in digital form. Many times the term eBook is used in place of "white paper" for the same style of document from a content marketing perspective. eBooks can be pretty much of any length, from 10 to 300 pages or even more. When using them for content marketing, most people keep them on the shorter side.

3. Podcasts

A podcast is an episodic program delivered through the Internet . They can consist of audio, video, text, or a combination of the three. The term is a blend of "broadcast" and "iPod" as podcasts became extremely popular with Apple's release of the iPod. Applications such as iTunes make downloading and subscribing to podcasts fast and easy. Downloading the latest release becomes an automatic process through these tools and makes it a great way to automatically distribute your message to your customers on a continuous basis.

4. Corporate Videos and Webinars

Corporate videos is a general terms that is used to describe a video that is used as a business tools rather than one that is used for entertainment. There are many reasons to produce a corporate video, but they usually fall within two camps:

Training Videos

Video is a great medium to educate people about your product, service, or the state of your industry. Many highly technical products are easier to understand when presented in video rather than just an article or in audio. You might want to train your customers or third parties that sell and service your product or service. You might also be surprised that many people will go through your training videos before they purchase your product or service, turning it into a sales tool.

Marketing and Promotional Videos

Today, most videos are made for online distribution through websites, video-sharing sites and social networks. Videos can be something as simple as you explaining your online software with screen capture software, using a webcam to record yourself talking, to a full blown production with cast and crew.

Webinars are a combination of the words "web" and "seminar" and are video presentations, lectures, or workshops that are transmitted over the web. The key feature of a webinar is its interactive elements. Users have the ability to give and receive feedback on the presentation. This interaction makes them slightly different from other forms of video. Many people record these webinars as well and make them available to view after the event has taken place.

5. Newsletters and Emails

E-mail and newsletters have been the granddaddy of content marketing for a long time. Many companies that don't even have blogs will send out the occasional newsletter or update. Usually, with e-mail, you want to have a limited amount of content with a call to action to drive the user to your website.

Developing your e-mail list through your website is of upmost importance. It allows you to have an ongoing relationship with your potential or existing customers and keep them updated on your products or services. Remember, you can also segment your email list in all sorts of different ways and send custom-targeted emails to your different audiences.

There is a wide variety of inexpensive services that will allow any company to send out e-mails quickly and easily. The two leaders in the space are

ConstantContact com and MailChimp.com. They offer starter plans for free, so there is little reason not to try adding e-mail to your content marketing strategy.

6. Case Studies

Studies Case studies are very effective marketing tools for all businesses. They highlight a satisfied customer that uses your product or service in a positive, real-world scenario. They're usually is only a page or two in a narrative form and clearly illustrate a problem and a solution with a testimonial and a light amount of data or charts to easily demonstrate the effectiveness of your product or service at a glance.

Many companies these days are now doing video case studies on their clients. These are admittedly a bit harder to do because you need to get your client physically involved, but they are more powerful than a standard text-based case study because your client delivers the message directly.

7. Online Training

Many products and service are complex to use and have a steep learning curve. Online training and education is a great way to explain these products and services in video, text and self-paced tutorials.

AdWords is Google's advertising product where people can buy text ads on Google next to search results. It can be a fairly complex product to use, and Google has done a great job making free, extensive training available to anyone. You don't even need to be an existing advertiser ; all videos are available to the public.

All of this content helps educate people both pre- and post-sale. Many people are cautious and want to fully learn about and understand a product before committing to it.

8. Customer Service

In a lot of ways , customer service IS content marketing. You're trying to serve your customers all the information they need regardless of where they are within the sales cycle. You're trying to educate them and get them to either make a purchase or remain a customer. Your customer service strategy will fall under two different approaches: proactive and reactive.

Proactive Customer Service

With a proactive approach, you are trying to anticipate the needs of your customers. You are trying to provide them with as much information as you can about your product so that they can educate themselves and solve their own customer service issues without having to contact your company. Many people would rather head over to your website than pick up the phone and call your company.

One company that does proactive customer service right is GE's appliance division. In the major appliances category, the ASCI survey has named General Electric number one in customer service. They anticipate the potential problems and questions their customers might have with an appliance and offer solutions and information online.

Reactive Customer Service

Many times customers do not want to spend time reading the available customer service information and will want to communicate with you directly. The Internet is a wide-open place, and if you don't give your customers open avenues of communication, they will hold the conversation elsewhere on the web. There are many different avenues available for communication, either public or private, that you can choose to support.

Here are just a few of the available options:

-Have a Contact Us form on your website.

-Have Voice and email option.

-Have website chat.

-Have community forums: Forums are a great way to provide customer service in an open and public way. This also allows others to view previous support occurrences. Many companies also find community members will sometimes help and answer each other's questions.

-Social Media Options: People these days expect companies to provide customer service through social media. Many companies develop customer services teams that specifically monitor and help support customers on social channels.

Chapter Six: Using Social Media To Your Greatest Advantage To Market Your Content

1. How To Use Facebook To Market Your Content

Facebook is one of the most popular social media platforms today with over one billion users actively using it worldwide on a daily basis. There are many companies and affiliate marketers that have used Facebook to their advantage by actively marketing on it using certain marketing strategies. In this chapter you will learn how to market on Facebook effectively while becoming a popular online presence on this social media platform.

Effective Facebook Marketing Strategy

In order to market effectively on Facebook, there will be a few steps that you will need to follow in order to make sure you build your presence on the platform without being considered as spam.

Step One: Differentiate Between Whether You Want To Market With Business Pages, Ads or Through Facebook Groups

This will be an important step you will need to follow because every option that is available to you will require you to market it differently. There are many advantages and disadvantages to marketing these different profiles and knowing them will help you determine which we be the best for you to market.

1. Marketing Facebook Pages

Advantages: Pages are free to set up as they can be easily created and accessed through your primary Facebook profile and pages are relatively easy to set up.

Disadvantages: It can be difficult to set up a fan base with a Facebook page. You will need to work hard and consistently to build up a fan base.

2. Marketing Facebook Ads

Advantages: The ads that you create have extremely powerful targeting parameters, which means that you can target whatever size audience you want to target.

Disadvantages: Depending on what your overall goals are, marketing these ads can become quite expensive in the long run.

3. Marketing in Facebook Groups

Advantages: Marketing in Facebook Groups is something that is free to do and groups tend to have high levels on engagement.

Disadvantages: Marketing through this avenue can become very time consuming, which many people are not willing to do.

Marketing With Facebook Pages

As stated above marketing on Facebook through the use of Facebook pages is one of the easiest and simplest ways that you can market on Facebook today. However, it is hard to build a presence on Facebook using this marketing method. If you decide to market as an affiliate market there are many ways that you can make sure that you do it effectively.

1. Customize Your Page Cover Image and Profile Picture

If you have a custom logo that you like to use, you will want to set that up as your main profile picture. It's as simple as that.

Your cover image will be a whole different ball game. You will have to choose for yourself what you will want to use to fill up that space such as money or pictures of the product you are promoting.

2. Fill Out The About Section

This section of your Facebook page is the place where you will want to sell yourself or the product you are promoting to those who visit your page. This is your chance to improve visitors and perhaps even make a couple of sales in the process.

In this section you will want to make sure that you put plenty of good information such as what your company or affiliate program is all about, why your program or company is different from the rest and other important details that you may want to share with your visitors. If you have enough time try to write the About section with your specific targeted audience in mind.

If you have a website or blog this section can be easily created because all that you have to do is copy and paste what you have on your blog straight to this section if you prefer. Regardless of what you decide to do make sure to create this section in a friendly and helpful manner. Whatever you do, do not try to sell your product right off the bat as people are most likely to turn away from your page rather then spend time visiting it. Make it a habit to help people rather than straight up sell to them.

3. Post Helpful and Useful Information To Your Wall On A Daily Basis

If there is one thing most audience's love, it is consistency and relevant information. As such you will want to make it a habit to post relevant and helpful information for your visitors to see on a daily basis. Some of the things that you may want to post regularly can include:

- Links to your blog posts if you have a blog.
- Links to any articles that you may have personally written.
- Coupons or savings codes for the products you are promoting.
- New announcements pertaining to your product or affiliate network.
- Helpful insights that will help your visitors.

4. Do Not Spam Your Wall

If there is one thing that will get you flagged by Facebook as a spam page is by you constantly spamming your wall with posts such as "Buy this now" or "make money online this way." I know that while you are in the game to make money on whatever product you are promoting or by promoting your affiliate network, you will need to resist the urge to spam constantly.

Before posting any new information to your wall, stop and ask yourself if the content you are putting up with me insightful and relevant to what your audience is looking for. If so then post it but if it doesn't, don't risk it. Spamming your wall with useless content will only work to drive your visitors away, not to keep them engaged in what you have to say.

Marketing With Facebook Ads

When it comes to use Facebook ads in your marketing methods, there are several different ads that you can choose from. Each type of ad that you can market with will have different outcomes and will range in price depending on what you need. You can create an ad directly linked to your Facebook Page that you are building an audience for or an ad that will drive traffic directly to your website or blog.

When choosing to market your product or affiliate network with Facebook ads, you will be given the chance to use Facebook's most powerful audience-targeting tool. With this tool you can literally find a large audience to target your ads too based upon whatever you wish. You can narrow down your audience to specific age, location, what their interests are or even what zip code they are in.

Regardless of the kind of audience you are looking to target, you will be able to customize your Facebook ads according to this audience. Keep in mind that the more ads you have to target different demographic groups, the better results you are going to have.

For example, let's say you want to target baseball fans. If this is your goal it is highly recommend that you create ads for every type of baseball team out there, giving yourself the chance to gain an audience from across the MLB league. Regardless of the kind of ads you wish to create or the specific niche that you want to target, make sure that you take the time to research high quality and relevant keywords to help target your ads accordingly.

2. Using Twitter To Your Advantage

As of late 2013, Twitter has been estimated to have nearly 53 millions users worldwide that use this social platform on a daily basis. With numbers like this, it makes Twitter one of the most ideal places to market your affiliate product or network. It is such a great place to market that you may be very surprised by how you can utilize the 140 character website to drive a flood of traffic to your sales page on a daily basis.

So, how can you improve your Twitter presence to drive high quality traffic to your sales page and drive more commission payments into your pocket? Here are a few simple tips that you can use to leverage the power of Twitter for your online affiliate business.

1. Make Sure That You Optimize Your Profile On Twitter

To optimize your profile on Twitter effectively, you will want to make sure that both your voice and online presence are branded well together. The best way to do this is to make sure that your bio and tweets have the same kind of voice on a consistent basis and that your tweets reflect what your online affiliate business is all about.

Also make sure that you personalize your bio by adding a link to your sales page or website and giving a clear explanation about who you are and what your company is all about.

2. Make Sure To Communicate With Those Who Are Considered Experts In Your Niche On Twitter and Learn From Them

There is nothing better than learning from those who are already successfully marketing on Twitter. While Twitter itself can seem like a massive platform so finding these experts can become a small challenge. However, to make this task easier simply use the search tool and search for high quality and relevant keywords in your niche and you will be able to narrow down popular users in that particular area.

As soon as you find these users I highly recommend that you begin communicating with them on a daily basis and follow them. They may post tweets once in a while that you will find extremely helpful and may want to implement into your own marketing campaign.

3. Tweet As Regularly As Possible

Similar to Facebook marketing, the key to success is to post on a consistent and regular basis. Tweeting as often as possible is the sign of an active profile and this is something that followers look for. When posting tweets to your profile, make sure that they are relevant to your niche, high quality content that you know your followers will click on and is content that will get a bunch of retweets.

Consistency is key to be a successful Twitter marketer. Tweeting only once a week or once a month will do nothing but guarantee that you fail in this marketing venture. You want to make sure that you stay on top of your followers minds instead of them just forgetting about you.

4. Regularly Favorite Tweets and Retweet As Often As You Can

If you want to catch the eye of potential followers, then do not be afraid to favorite a tweet or retweet something they have posted. Retweeting is a great way to help you link to relevant posts within the industry and can even go a long way in helping to showcase you as a leader in the field.

Favoriting tweets on the other hand have more power and pull on audiences as this is something that many marketers are not aware of when they first begin marketing on Twitter. This will immediately get you noticed on Twitter by your followers and can even help you gain more followers in the long run.

5. Follow The Latest Trends and Hashtags As Often As Possible

There is a specific section within Twitter where you can see exactly what is trending on Twitter in real time. Following this real time trends will give you the chance to make connections with the accounts that are trending so that you can make your brand stand out.

My recommendation is to tweet relevant tweets alongside the trending topics as people will see your tweet whenever they search for a specific hashtag. When you tag your tweets with relevant hashtags, you'll give yourself the chance to gain new followers. However, make sure that you use them only sparingly as people may consider it as spam if they are attached to content that is completely irrelevant.

6. Take Advantage of Promoted Tweets

Not sure what promoted tweets are? Well, they are tweets that you ordinarily create and then pay a certain amount to promote it to a specific target audience. Taking advantage of this promotion within Twitter is a great way to target an audience of your choice. However, in order to make sure you get the most out of your promoted tweets make sure that you do not tweet anything that may be considered too spammy or a tweet that tricks people to click on a link.

Remember, keep your tweets fresh and try not to let any tweets that you promote to run for a long period of time. Keep it short and simple and you'll be able to attract new followers to your account.

7. Don't Forget To Use Images and Videos To Your Advantage

Whenever you use images or videos, you will be driving even more traffic to your sales page or website. It has been shown that by using videos and images, affiliate marketers are able to gain at least 3 to 4 times more clicks on their links than marketers who don't utilize them.

You will begin to notice that after a while, plain tweets are just that: plain. While you may be engaging your followers with relevant and insightful content, it will begin to get boring after a while. Adding images and videos to your current tweets will give them richer quality which has been proven to have your followers interact with you more often and will reduce the risk of you receiving negative feedback or comments.

3. The Power of Reddit

While many people know of Facebook and Twitter and assume that those are the most powerful social media networking websites online today, many people are unfamiliar with Reddit. As an active and daily user on Reddit myself, I can testify to how effective this social media website is from a marketing standpoint.

If you are not sure what Reddit is, it is simply a social media networking site where users can submit links to picture or websites with other members of the community to share it with. If used correctly you can gain a lot of traffic from Reddit. In order to do it correctly you will need to learn how to market, without marketing. Confusing, I know but this is something you will need to learn and you will need to learn it fast.

The thing is when it comes to using Reddit as a source of marketing, the website has one rule that most marketers have a problem adhering to: No self-promotion. This can be especially tricky if you want to gain traffic to a website or sales page, but just because it is tricky that does not mean it is impossible to do.

Here are a few tips and tricks that you can use to utilize Reddit and to drive lots of traffic to your product sales page or affiliate network page.

Tips To Marketing Successfully On Reddit

1. Build Up Your Karma

Your karma standing on Reddit will give users an idea of how active you are within the community. There are several ways that you can build up your karma such as commenting on other posts, upvoting posts and sharing good links with others in the community. While this may not necessarily increase the ranking of the posts that you share compared to a member who just recently joined, it will go a long way in helping you to improve your status among other "Redditors."

2. Use The Sub-Reddits As Wisely As Possible

When it comes to finding areas within Reddit to post in that fits nicely within your niche, you will need to learn how to use the sub-reddit section. However, there have been times where even I have found the subreddit section to be a tad bit more targeted than I would like. You can find a subreddit category in practically every niche whether it is gaming, copywriting or politics. The key is narrowing down the categories to fit into your needs.

Do your research ahead of time and spend some time going through all of the subreddits to narrow down the ones that will best fit into your needs and that will help drive a lot of traffic to your sales page or website.

3. Post Unique Stories or Links Only

The one reason why many people continue going to Reddit on a daily basis is to find unique, hilarious, cute or inspiring stories or pictures from other users. Remember, this site is a sharing website and the more funny and unique things that you share on it, the more popular you will become on it.

As a user myself I can tell you that I could spend hours on Reddit just looking for things to click on. Can you see where this can come in handy as an affiliate marketer? If you post great content and links to the site and other users like what you post, the more upvotes you will gain and the higher up your link will appear on the website.

Conclusion

Throughout this book, I have tried to highlight the importance of high-quality content. I have done this not because I'm a stickler for the rules but because these practices work. I have seen positive results time and again in my own businesses and in those of my clients, and I am confident that, if you implement the strategies I have presented in this guide, you will also see success.

A successful digitally marketed business is not something that happens on its own, and it is not something that you can create overnight. However, as I hope you have seen from what I have presented in this book, setting up a high-quality site and promoting it is not as difficult as you might expect. With a little know-how and the proper tools, you will be able to turn your passion into reality—a high-earning site that captures the attention of visitors and converts them into paying customers eager to put money in your pocket each and every day.

Of course, none of us truly knows what the future holds. A few years ago, the Internet was a very different place, and successful businesses used different strategies in order to succeed. Social media has been a game-changer. Blogging has become more sophisticated and will continue to evolve. In a few years, digital marketing may be very different than it is today, but I am confident that the basic ideas I have outlined in this book will serve you well in the changing landscape of Internet Marketing.

To hear about Entrepreneur Publishing's new books first (and to be notified when there are free promotions), sign up to their New Release Mailing List.

Finally, if you enjoyed this book, please take the time to share your thoughts and post a review on Amazon. It'd be greatly appreciated!

Thank you and good luck!

Preview Of 'Speed Reading For Entrepreneurs: Seven Speed Reading Tactics To Read Faster, Improve Memory And Increase Profits' from Entrepreneur Publishing

Tip 1: Choosing Material Selectively

In order to speed read effectively, there are a few things we need to do before we begin learning the techniques. By doing a little prep work, you can maximize your potential and learn at a steady pace. The faster you master the techniques, the faster you can start doing more for your business to maximize profits.

First, decide what you want to read about. Make a list of a few topics that you plan on becoming more knowledgeable about and why they will be beneficial to your business. If you were having problems getting things done on time, a book or article series on time management would be beneficial. If you're trying to maximize your marketing efforts or looking to cut costs in your advertising, there are a wealth of informative articles and books available to you. Make a list of at least five topics you want to learn about, or areas you want to improve your business.

After making your list, take a good look at what you have written. Some of the subjects, no doubt, will require more research than others, and some subjects will require specific books or technical manuals. You want to make sure when you're reading for entrepreneurial gain, that you're reading the right materials. If you're looking for advice or tips, informal articles and blog posts are all right, but technical knowledge or skills will usually require you to purchase a book.

With your list in sight, try to narrow your search even further. If you're looking to maximize revenue through marketing, try and be specific on what kind of marketing, such as business to business or email marketing. Knowing exactly what you're looking for is key to absorbing quality material. You can read as quickly as you want, but if you're not reading the right thing you won't benefit from any of the material.

Another technique you can employ is to pick reading materials that correspond with the type of materials you are trying to produce. If you're trying to up the number of views you receive on your blog each month, try reading articles and blog posts. If you're looking to write better eBooks, try reading those instead of scanning endless blogs and articles. If it's an actual novel you're looking to write, then you should invest a little time and money into acquiring an actual paperback or hardback copy of a book that you think is relevant to you and your needs. Doing this allows you to look not only the content, but the formatting and vernacular people in your desired field are using to find success. The goal here is to pick your content based on quality not quantity, since this program is designed to make it so you read less overall. The better the information in the first place, the less extra reading you have to do.

An easy way to organize your reading materials is to make piles in order of importance. You can always print blog posts, articles, or emails, so this should not be an issue for you. Print whatever you are wanting to read, and make three piles: Most Important, Moderately Important, Least Important. Reading the most important materials first is vital because your mind is ready to process information at the beginning of your reading session. As you progress, your retention and attention to detail wanes, so you want to make sure the information you get early on is of the most value to you.

Remember, one of the biggest mistakes prospective speed readers make is to try and read as much material as possible once they pick up speed. While you can always read more, the goal is that as a business person you plan on reading less so you can do more, and that means that you need to pick the right quality and the right type of reading material to learn what you need to learn to reach your goals.

Click here to check out the rest of Speed Reading For Entrepreneurs: Seven Speed Reading Tactics To Read Faster, Improve Memory And Increase Profits on Amazon.

Or go to: http://amzn.to/1FdMcU7

More Books for Entrepreneurs

Click here to check out the rest of Entrepreneur Publishing's books on Amazon. Below you'll find some of my other popular books that are popular on Amazon and Kindle as well. Simply click on the links below to check them out. Alternatively, you can visit my author page on Amazon to see other work done by me.

How Audiobooks Make You Smarter: 7 Little Known Ways Audio Books Can Boost Memory Capacity And Increase Intelligence

How To Write A Book And Publish On Amazon: Make Money With Amazon Kindle, CreateSpace And Audiobooks

Gardening For Entrepreneurs: Gardening Techniques For High Yield, High Profit Crops

Speed Reading For Entrepreneurs: Seven Speed Reading Tactics To Read Faster, Improve Memory And Increase Profits

If the links do not work, for whatever reason, you can simply search for these titles on the Amazon website to find them.